THE NATURE OF
CARIBOU

H. JOHN RUSSELL

THE NATURE OF
CARIBOU

SPIRIT OF THE NORTH

GREYSTONE BOOKS

Douglas & McIntyre

Vancouver/Toronto

PAGES II–III

Reindeer travel the
Arctic snows of spring.
BJÖRN RÖHSMAN/

NATURFOTOGRAFERNA

PAGE IV

A barren-ground caribou
male. LEONARD LEE RUE III

Text copyright © 1998 by H. John Russell
Photographs copyright © 1998 by the photographers credited
98 99 00 01 02   5 4 3 2 1

All rights reserved. No part of this book may be reproduced, stored in a retrieval system or transmitted, in any form or by any means, without the prior written permission of the publisher or, in the case of photocopying or other reprographic copying, a licence from CANCOPY (Canadian Reprography Collective), Toronto, Ontario.

Greystone Books
A division of Douglas & McIntyre Ltd.
1615 Venables Street
Vancouver, British Columbia v5L 2H1

Originated by Greystone Books and published simultaneously in the United States of America by Sierra Club Books, San Francisco.

CANADIAN CATALOGUING IN PUBLICATION DATA

Russell, H. John, 1944–
    The nature of caribou

ISBN 1-55054-622-8

    1. Caribou. 2. Caribou—Pictorial works. I. Title.
QL737.U55R87 1998   599.65'8   C98-910025-1

Jacket and book design by Isabelle Swiderski
Editing by Nancy Flight
Front jacket photograph by Denver Bryan
Back jacket photograph by Matthias Breiter
Printed and bound in Hong Kong by C & C Offset Printing Co., Ltd.

The publisher gratefully acknowledges the assistance of the Canada Council and of the British Columbia Ministry of Tourism, Small Business and Culture. The publisher also acknowledges the financial support of the Government of Canada through the Book Publishing Industry Development Program for its publishing activities.

CONTENTS

PREFACE

Caribou, especially barren-ground caribou, have occupied most of my biological career. Flying in a small, fixed-wing aircraft, I have followed them along their migration paths, watched them on their winter and summer ranges and marked the progress of their calving. I have also been with them on the ground, in the peaceful wilderness in which they live. These were precious times, when I could really see the microhabitats they use and observe subtle behavioural nuances that are impossible to observe from the air.

I have come to greatly love this animal. This is not a scientific response, but it takes one into a realm that is equally rewarding, if not more so. In this book I hope to transmit some of my own understanding of caribou, along with scientific and cultural knowledge provided by others.

The caribou is an animal of many adaptations that lives happily in very cold, harsh conditions. It lives in partnership with the wolf, forming an ecosystem that functions best when the two species are allowed to respond to the climate, which determines how much food the caribou have to eat. Climate can create a drought, which decreases the amount of food, or it can cover plentiful food with too much snow. Climate, caribou and wolf create a dance that has been going on for thousands of years and will go on for many more, if we make wise economic and political decisions.

I hope that this book will give readers a greater understanding and appreciation of caribou. I know that writing it has done so for me.

FACING PAGE

The extra-long legs—a quarter hidden by long grass—of this yearling wild forest reindeer help it move through deep snow in winter. ANTTI LEINONEN

THIS BOOK IS DEDICATED TO THE PEOPLE OF OLD CROW

ACKNOWLEDGEMENTS

I wish to thank my partner, Valerie Haig-Brown, for being there and for all the support and encouragement she has given me in my efforts to write. She also went over the first drafts with a very skilled pen. My brother, Dick Russell, and Jan Edmunds also made many suggestions after the first version of the manuscript.

I want to thank my mother and dad, Kay and Andy Russell, for sparking my interest in the outdoors and nature. My appreciation also goes to Ron Jakimchuk for having faith in me all these years and for getting me there, and to Gordon Hartman for his humour and many helpful conversations. George Calef and I shared ideas in the glow of many midnight suns and northern lights.

I am indebted to the caribou gurus, Dave Klein and Tom Bergerud, for teaching with zest and listening with a critical ear. Thanks to Serge Couturier, Stu Luttich, Jim Schaeffer, Rick Farnell, Ken Whitten, Ray Cameron, Jim Davis, Guy St. Marten, Rick Brown, Len Sopuck and the many other biologists that I've worked alongside in the field.

Finally, my editor, Nancy Flight, has been most helpful in creating this book.

FACING PAGE

A young female caribou framed by the red leaves of dwarf birch. RICK MCINTYRE

PAGES XII–XIII

Denali National Park, with its combination of Arctic and mountain scenery, is a splendid backdrop for Rangifer tarandus granti, *the western version of the barren-ground caribou*. MATTHIAS BREITER

THE GIFT

Part One

OF CARIBOU

The caribou is one of the most beautiful animals in the world. Watching a herd of caribou trot or prance across the tundra, one is struck by their grace, speed and carefree spirit. They even seem to have a sense of humour. Somehow managing to appear both regal and silly at the same time, they evoke a combination of love and mirth in the observer.

Caribou are native to much of the tundra, forest and alpine areas of the Northern Hemisphere, living between 47 and 82 degrees latitude. Many caribou herds migrate between winter and summer ranges, sometimes up to a thousand kilometres (600 miles) each way. They serve as an extremely important resource to northern peoples, including the Inuit, Dene and Cree, the Sámi of Lapland, and the Koryaks, Chukchi and other deer people of northern Russia.

Caribou belong to the deer family. Like all members of this family, they grow and shed their antlers each year. Caribou are the only species, however, in which both sexes grow antlers. They normally live between seven and twelve years. Females live longer; ten-year-old males are very rare.

All caribou, including reindeer, belong to one species, *Rangifer tarandus*. The word "reindeer" refers to both domestic and wild caribou populations in Europe and Asia. Although caribou look quite different in different parts of the world, genetic variations are so small that all caribou can interbreed easily. The variations are the result of adaptations to particular local environments.

Until near the end of the last glaciation, about twelve thousand years ago, there

FACING PAGE

A prancing Peary caribou. This animal is adapted to wolf predation by being a light-footed, streamlined runner and to extreme cold by having a compact body.

JIM BRANDENBURG/
MINDEN PICTURES

1

were many more species of large vegetarian mammals using the habitats of the Northern Hemisphere than there are now. Species such as the mammoth, mastodon and shrub ox (a relative of the muskox) lived with the caribou and muskox in still-productive patches of land between the ice sheets. As the ice began to melt, these other species became extinct, emptying the niches they occupied. Some of the subspecies of caribou today may be attempts to fill those emptied niches. Others are filling new niches that were created as the ice retreated, baring large tracts of land.

The seven main subspecies of caribou are two types of barren-ground caribou, Peary caribou, woodland caribou, wild and domestic reindeer, wild forest reindeer and Svalbard reindeer. Part 2 describes the barren-ground caribou, which are by far the largest in number of the caribou subspecies. The rest of Part 1 describes the other subspecies of caribou.

POPULATIONS EXCEEDING 100,000 ANIMALS*

1 • Western Arctic herd: 550,000; 2 • Porcupine herd: 150,000; 3 • Bluenose herd: 120,000; 4 • Bathurst herd: 350,000; 5 • Beverly herd: 285,000; 6 • Qamanirjuaq herd: 495,000; 7 • Leaf River herd: 300,000; 8 • George River herd: 700,000; 9 • Taimyr Peninsula herd: 600,000

POPULATIONS IN RUSSIA ESTIMATED AT 40,000 TO 100,000 ANIMALS*

10 • Lena-Olenek herd: 80,000; 11 • Yana-Indigirka herd: 40,000; 12 • Sundrum herd: 85,000

*most recent estimates

Peary caribou
*(Rangifer tarandus
pearyi)*

Barren-ground caribou
*(Rangifer tarandus
groenlandicus* and
*Rangifer tarandus
granti). R. t. granti*
live in Alaska and
northern Yukon
(Porcupine herd).

Woodland caribou
*(Rangifer tarandus
caribou)*

Reindeer, both wild
and domestic *(Rangifer
tarandus tarandus)*

Wild forest reindeer
*(Rangifer tarandus
fennicus)*

Svalbard reindeer
*(Rangifer tarandus
platyrhynchus)*

Elizabeth Islands is bare soil or rock, and the climate is so severe that plants can't get a foothold in many parts. When they do they may be weakened or killed by being grazed. This is true for any plant, but plants in the High Arctic are among the most marginal of any in the world. Because grazing jeopardizes the very substance the caribou depend upon, they follow a careful grazing strategy to minimize this problem. Much of the time they too are on the edge of survival.

As spring arrives, the light becomes intense; the sun shines for twenty-four hours a day, turning the snow into a glaring sheet. But the ridges quickly become bare, allowing the ground there to thaw and plants to begin to grow. At this time, females migrate to their calving areas in their summer ranges, which are often near the northern coasts of their respective islands. They may also travel to another island up to 100 kilometres (60 miles) across the sea ice. These moves are part of a strategy to conserve the plants the caribou will depend on during the winter. They seek out snow-free ridge slopes on their calving ground and then expand their grazing as snow disappears elsewhere. Males usually move to similar summer ranges. The sedges, grasses and flowering plants, such as the purple saxifrage, that they feed on during summer are least vulnerable to grazing because they are often in the lushest parts of the ranges and recover fastest. In the later part of the summer and in the fall, the caribou strip the leaves off arctic willow before they turn but after they have served the plants' purpose. The caribou leave the twigs, which will be used for winter feed.

Some years only 50 per cent of the ground is bared before the snow starts to fall and frost enters the few centimetres of surface soil above the permafrost. These are not good years for the caribou, since they have little time and few resources to gain strength to get through the next winter. Ice storms in the fall may coat the flattened plants of this stark land with several centimetres of ice. As a result, the plants are very hard to get at the following winter, and the caribou are forced to spend much more

ALL THOSE WHO KNOW THE PLIGHT OF THE PEARY CARIBOU FEAR THAT IT MAY BECOME EXTINCT.

energy than in normal winters pawing through the icy crust. During such winters many caribou perish, especially young ones. The population may then be devastated for several years to come, since it takes that long for females to regain the general body condition and fat reserves required to become pregnant. Surviving caribou may be fairly old before they can produce any young to replace themselves.

During the past four decades the number of Peary caribou has dropped from about twenty-six thousand animals to two thousand. They originally dwindled to two thousand by 1985, and then the population tripled on some islands by 1993. Then three bad winters back to back again reduced the caribou to two thousand.

There are several possible reasons that the caribou have not been able to regain their population size of the 1960s. One possible cause is the fallout from atomic bomb testing in the fifties. Another is the persistent pesticides that get swept up off lakes and carried northward in the upper atmosphere and then dropped by winds descending in the polar region. Once the maverick ions from the fallout or molecules from the pesticides get into the tissues of an animal, they can affect its cellular activity and metabolism in unpredictable ways. Still another cause of the drop in population may be increased numbers of wolves supported by high numbers of muskoxen. Finally, caribou may not be adapted to the climate changes in the area caused by increased greenhouse gases in the earth's atmosphere.

Many who know the plight of the Peary caribou fear that it may become extinct. The Peary caribou is listed as an endangered species under the Endangered Species Act of Canada. The Northwest Territories government and the Inuit are trying to develop a strategy for ensuring that this subspecies will continue to live in the High Arctic in spite of increasing pressure for industrial development and the local need for protein. To solve the latter problem, band councils fly hunters to hunting grounds farther south, where the caribou are not endangered, or buy caribou meat from these areas.

WOODLAND CARIBOU

Woodland caribou live in the boreal forests that stretch across the subarctic lowlands of North America. The boreal forest is also known as the taiga. Generally, this forest is sparse and boggy in the north. In the south, the forest is thicker and the ground is firmer.

In North America the most southerly populations of caribou are all woodland and occur in four provinces. In British Columbia the International herd is found in the Selkirk Mountains south of Nelson and extends into Idaho a short distance. In Ontario there are about a hundred caribou on the Slate Islands near the north shore of Lake Superior. In Quebec the Grands Jardins herd lives just east of Quebec City, and in Newfoundland there is a small herd on the Avalon Peninsula south of St. John's.

Known as the grey ghosts of the forest, woodland caribou are notoriously difficult to find. They live in very small, scattered populations in which individuals and small groups are often on the move, though they usually do not migrate long distances between summer and winter ranges. If they are in one place one day, they cannot be relied upon to be there the next, especially if they have detected the presence of a predator or any other intruder. They avoid openings in the forest when they can, crossing roads quickly when necessary. They seem embarrassed when they know they are being observed. During spring and summer, you usually see only two caribou together; during mating, you see two to four together, and in winter, you tend to see six together.

Early one morning in July, when I was in a pine forest several kilometres south of Great Slave Lake in the Northwest Territories, I saw a movement out of the corner of my eye. As I turned, I saw three woodland caribou travelling quietly through the forest, angling towards me. I froze in order to let them pass undisturbed. In the lead was an adult female, followed by a calf and a yearling. As they were about to pass by, the mother spotted me and stopped. They all looked at me and soon resumed their silent pace, which seemed like a casual walk, but in an instant they were out of sight. It had all happened so fast and with so little fanfare that I could have persuaded myself that I had imagined the entire encounter. But the forest floor of sparsely covered sand showed their footprints quite clearly.

Woodland caribou depend on large tracts of old-growth coniferous forests, where there is little moose habitat. (Moose habitat is composed of willow and deciduous trees, which grow in recent burns and disturbed sites such as riverbeds and logging areas.) Moose don't make good neighbours for caribou. Several moose living in an area will attract and support wolves, which then may prey on caribou they stumble across. The caribou, being small, are easy to kill if the wolves catch them in vulnerable situations—for example, in crusted snow or when their energy reserves are low. The wolves, however, have a great deal of energy, thanks to moose meat subsidies.

Woodland caribou live off sparse shrubs, such as willow, birch and blueberry, that form the undergrowth of their forest home. They also eat the grasses, sedges and flowering plants that grow there thinly. Boreal forests often have a lichen mat understorey, and the limbs and bark of the trees also bear arboreal lichens, which the caribou resort to, especially in winters when the snow is deep.

A viable woodland caribou population can be very small and dispersed, provided that few die each year, because few calves are born to a small population. When it is time to give birth, mothers space themselves far apart so that predators

KNOWN AS THE

GREY GHOSTS

OF THE FOREST,

WOODLAND CARIBOU

ARE NOTORIOUSLY

DIFFICULT TO FIND.

FACING PAGE
A woodland caribou bull in typical winter habitat in British Columbia. To deal with the deep snow of the forests it needs long legs and snowshoe feet.
MICHAEL H. FRANCIS

cannot find a target area to search for calves. Each female will calve in a bog by herself well away from any other caribou, nursing the calf when it needs to nurse and feeding near it as it sleeps. Until the calf is fully mobile, about a week after birth, the mother moves around as little as possible to decrease the chances that a predator will cross her scent trail.

In Eurasia, Alaska and Canada, the forest industry is aggressively logging old-growth forests, and woodland caribou are particularly vulnerable. Over the next several decades, in a large-scale experiment, Canadian forest companies and provincial governments are planning to log virtually all of the southern part of the boreal forest. Because these trees grow so slowly, this kind of logging is more like mining than husbandry. The forest companies claim that they can maintain caribou at present numbers by controlling when areas are cut and how large the cut blocks are.

Such a large-scale operation has never been tried before. For this reason, when the officials involved claim they are completely confident that this management will be successful, we need to be cautious about believing them. In making this claim, they are suggesting that they know all the biological requirements of this subspecies, given any kind of winter conditions and any other crises the species may experience over the decades. They are also suggesting that they can reproduce these requirements in the logged areas. Both of these suggestions are questionable. For instance, Ontario biologists think they can allow logging with a 40-year cut cycle. But biologists in Alberta say that it takes 150 years to produce enough lichen for hard winters, since caribou go to 150- to 250-year-old forests in winters of deep snow.

Mountain Caribou

The mountain caribou is a variant of the woodland caribou and is similar in size, colour and genetics. Mountain caribou tend to have larger antlers than the woodland caribou, however, and unlike the woodland caribou, the mountain caribou always migrate between summer and winter ranges. They spend the winter in the forest, as their woodland counterparts do, but because they live in the mountains, they calve in alpine meadows rather than in bogs.

Both these caribou have long legs, which enable them to move around in the deep snow that builds up in their winter ranges. Because of their long legs, they are sometimes mistaken for moose, especially in their antlerless state.

The migrations of mountain caribou are usually less than 50 kilometres (30 miles) between summer range and wintering ground. These migrations usually involve elevation changes of at least 300 metres (1000 feet). Not all mountain caribou spend the entire winter in forest. A few populations in British Columbia and Yukon spend at least a part of each winter on high tundra plateaus. Here they are more visible to human hunters, who can travel more easily on wind-packed snow than on the deep, soft snow in forests. Some of these populations have disappeared, possibly because of such vulnerability. Since they are small, most of these populations are very sensitive to even a slight increase in death rates. In Labrador at least one population, near Hart Lake, has almost disappeared, and another, in the Mealy Mountains, has not grown for many years when it should

IF THE SNOW MELTS
SOON ENOUGH,
FEMALES MIGRATE
TO THE HIGH
ALPINE CIRQUES
AND RIDGES JUST
BELOW THE PEAKS
OF THE MOUNTAINS
TO GIVE BIRTH.

Facing page

A mountain version of

woodland caribou gives

birth in an open glade.

GLEN AND REBECCA

GRAMBO

have, because, except for hunting, conditions have been good.

Most mountain caribou follow the same low-density, starve-the-predator strategy as their woodland relatives. In winter they spread themselves out in small groups of half a dozen or so in forest habitats on valley slopes and low plateaus. If the snow melts soon enough, females migrate to the high alpine cirques and ridges just below the peaks of the mountains to give birth. A few go to slightly lower locales near the timberline. Occupying these high, remote locations further reduces their exposure to predation, since predators travel valleys more than they do peaks and ridges. If there is deep snow and it melts late, females are forced to calve in the lowlands, where more of the calves succumb to predation.

Each population of caribou follows a strategy that is appropriate to the terrain and vegetation in its home range. For instance, two populations in central British Columbia separated by 320 kilometres (200 miles) use different elevations in early winter; the northern herd stays at higher elevations than the southern. They both prefer forests older than 140 years, but the southern herd uses cedar and hemlock forests and the northern herd uses balsam and spruce forests. Caribou eat arboreal lichen in both areas, but in the north they supplement it with blueberry and willow shrubs to increase the protein in their diet, while in the south they use false box, an evergreen broad-leafed shrub.

Such variability makes it hard to predict the needs of caribou in a particular area. Each population must be studied separately to know it beyond broad generalizations. This knowledge is necessary if logging or mining is planned in areas used by caribou. Fortunately, many governments have recognized this need and funded studies that have increased our understanding of these caribou tremendously in the last decade.

Newfoundland Caribou

Only the woodland subspecies lives on the island of Newfoundland. During the last great ice age, most of present-day Newfoundland was covered with ice; only small pieces of coastal margin on the tips of some peninsulas were exposed. Because the sea level was low, however, much of the continental shelf was dry land and there was a large refuge in the Grand Banks area. Today fishing nets occasionally bring in mammoth tusks, providing proof that in the past, instead of being a haven for cod, the Grand Banks supported these huge mammals. Mammoths preferred tundra habitat, suggesting that caribou could have survived there as well.

From 1900 to 1915, a large interior Newfoundland caribou herd numbered at least 40,000, but after that it rapidly declined and disappeared. Now several smaller populations of caribou total nearly 85,000 and are still increasing. They are of the woodland subspecies, having crossed from the mainland where that subspecies predominates. Newfoundland has the most southerly caribou in the world, on the Avalon Peninsula, just south of 47 degrees latitude, where they fluctuate in number between three and seven thousand over the years.

FACING PAGE

A male Newfoundland caribou of the woodland subspecies. There have never been wolves on the island, as is evident in the relatively bulky shape of this animal.

JOHN EASTCOTT/YVA MOMATIUK/HEDGEHOG HOUSE NEW ZEALAND

THE WILD FOREST

REINDEER IS

EXTREMELY LONG

LEGGED, ENABLING IT

TO TRAVEL THROUGH

THE DEEP SNOW IN

WINTER IN THE MOST

EASTERLY PARTS OF

FINLAND AND THE

KARELIAN DISTRICT

OF RUSSIA.

REINDEER

There are three subspecies of reindeer, all of which evolved in Eurasia. They are the wild reindeer, wild forest reindeer and Svalbard reindeer. Wild reindeer are similar to barren-ground caribou in habit, living in alpine and Arctic tundra during summer and usually the forests in winter. Wild forest reindeer are comparable to the woodland caribou in habit, and they have even longer legs to deal with deep snow. The Svalbard reindeer, mentioned earlier, almost went extinct before 1925, when Norway took on the governing of the Svalbard Islands and immediately banned all hunting of these reindeer. The population slowly grew to around fifteen hundred and has fluctuated around that number since then. Although some parts of the Svalbards are mountainous, these reindeer use the mid- to lower elevations. They are most similar in looks and genetics to Peary caribou, though they have larger legs and an even more rounded body.

A fence was erected along the eastern border of Finland to keep its domestic reindeer from straying into Russia and to keep wild reindeer and wild forest reindeer out of Finland. In spite of these best-laid plans, these reindeer managed to cross the fence from Russia's Kola Peninsula and repopulate parts of eastern Finland.

The wild forest reindeer is extremely long legged, enabling it to travel through the deep snow in winter in the most easterly parts of Finland and the Karelian district of Russia. It was hunted to extinction in Finland in about 1910 and almost wiped out in westernmost Russia, where reindeer herders saw the wild forest reindeer as competitors for the range their domestic herds depended on and therefore shot the animals at

FACING PAGE
A female and yearling wild reindeer. HANNU HAUTALA

PAGES 20–21
Silhouetted wild reindeer travelling along an Arctic shore in Scandinavia. HANNU HAUTALA

every opportunity. As reindeer husbandry decreased in the region, the number of wild forest reindeer began to increase and the animals moved back into Finland beginning in the 1940s. The numbers stabilized at around five thousand living on both sides of the border. It is heartening that this unusual subspecies has survived in the area of deep snow using habitat that no other subspecies of *Rangifer* could without aid from humans.

Russia supports large populations of migratory wild reindeer similar in habit to the barren-ground caribou. The largest of these, the Taimyr herd, calves on the Taimyr Peninsula, located about midway along the Arctic coast of Siberia, and is thought to number 600,000 animals. These reindeer winter in the forests south of the peninsula. They are important economically, since about 50,000 are harvested annually and sold to the meat shops of the large city of Norilsk and nearby towns. In the province of Yakutia, east of the Taimyr herd, there are three somewhat smaller herds, totalling at least 200,000 wild reindeer. In the first half of the century these four herds were declining, the result of overhunting and competition from domestic reindeer herds. Since the 1960s wild reindeer herds have regained their former high numbers of the previous century. Russian scientists believe that the numbers are up because people are becoming more centralized in and around the towns and cities and there are fewer domestic reindeer herds. Central and eastern Siberia also support many sedentary wild forest reindeer—possibly 60,000—in their taiga region.

In the far eastern portion of Siberia is the Kamchatka Peninsula, which lies west of the Bering Sea. This land is highly productive, capable of supporting healthy herds of reindeer. Historically, Kamchatka had three populations of a very large-bodied wild forest reindeer, but recently these populations have diminished in number, and two populations may have disappeared. One herd is partially protected by the Kronotsky Reserve but has been reduced from its former size by overhunting when it leaves the reserve.

The domestic reindeer is the husbanded version of the wild reindeer. The Sámi

FACING PAGE

This wild forest reindeer calf is less than a month old. ANTTI LEINONEN

ALTHOUGH THE

WILD CARIBOU AND

THE WOLF FORM A

HEALTHY ECOSYSTEM,

REINDEER HERDERS

SEE THE WOLF AS A

GREAT THREAT.

culture in northern Scandinavia is based on herding reindeer, though many people have adopted southern ways and move their animals to and from the summer range by truck. There are many herds of domestic reindeer in Norway, especially north of Trondheim. There are no wild reindeer in Sweden, but numerous domestic herds exist, all owned by law by descendants of the Sámi, as is the case in most of Norway. The Sámi have herded reindeer for thousands of years.

There are now domestic reindeer herds (the same subspecies as wild reindeer) across Scandinavia and Russia, a few in Alaska and one in Canada near Tuktoyaktuk. As mentioned earlier, there can be conflicts between domestic reindeer herders and wild members of the *Rangifer* species. The domestic herds need the same food and range as wild reindeer, so herders can feel threatened when a wild herd moves into the range they were counting on to feed their herd. In addition, although the wild caribou and the wolf form a healthy ecosystem, reindeer herders see the wolf as a great threat. In the past they shot the wild animals to solve these problems. Wild reindeer and wolves were almost completely wiped out of Scandinavia before they were protected in a few areas.

After the Chernobyl incident a cloud of radioactive dust spread northwest over Northern Europe, and many reindeer herds had to be slaughtered and the carcasses carefully disposed of. Now, more than a decade later, the levels of cesium are safe, reindeer herders can sell their stock, and domestic reindeer have returned to the numbers that existed before the Chernobyl incident. The situation changes during summers when there are large wild mushroom crops. Caribou/reindeer love mushrooms, which take up radioactive materials much more readily than do green plants.

In their entirety, all the caribou/reindeer populations in the world amount to a large number of animals. The wild populations total over four million, and there are at least half that many domestic reindeer. Their value to us in esthetic and economic terms is priceless; they are a most precious gift.

FACING PAGE

These domestic reindeer near Chukotka in eastern Russia include a few pinto and white animals, which are not common in domestic herds. STEVE KAUFMAN

An excitation leap is often triggered by the scent of a human or a predator. This leap plants a strong warning scent from the hind feet onto the ground for other caribou to pick up. MICHAEL H. FRANCIS

27

THE

Part Two

CARIBOU

YEAR

Now we come to the spectacular caribou populations that use the Arctic tundra and taiga of North America, the large migratory caribou herds—spectacular because of their long migrations and their huge numbers. There are six large populations of barren-ground caribou whose respective ranges slope southeast across the continent from between 64 and 71 degrees north latitude in northwestern Alaska to between 58 and 64 degrees on the west side of Hudson Bay. There are also two large woodland caribou populations ranging between 53 and 62 degrees north latitude on the Quebec and Labrador peninsula east of Hudson Bay that could easily be mistaken for barren-ground caribou. Although they are genetically woodland caribou, they look similar to and behave similarly to the barren-ground caribou. The large migratory wild reindeer herds that summer on the Siberian tundra and winter in its northern forest also fit the descriptions found in this chapter, with only minor differences in timing of events and latitudes occupied.

Other barren-ground caribou populations are smaller and have shorter migration routes. Those in central and southern Alaska and the northeastern part of the Northwest Territories, including Baffin Island, are examples. In the past some of these herds were quite large. Many of these populations have, in the past hundred years, gone through cycles from large to small and most are now large again. Only a few that are known to have been large are still small at present.

Barren-ground caribou have medium-sized bodies, and the males have the largest antlers of all caribou in length and width, a feature that makes the caribou

FACING PAGE

*This superb specimen of
the Denali herd displays
a beautifully even set of
antlers, a white yoke under
his throat and the beginning
of a white slash on his side.*

THOMAS MANGELSEN/

IMAGES OF NATURE

look almost out of proportion but at the same time regal. Probably the most spectacular aspect of these caribou is the size of the groups they may travel in. Spring migrations will occasionally induce them to travel in lines of several thousand animals that are many kilometres long. These populations migrate huge distances from their calving ground to the summer range and on to wintering areas. The distances require several days of sustained travel, and the animals travel many kilometres a day. Their domain, though not as severe as that of the Peary caribou, is one of low nutrients combined with low temperatures.

By far the largest groups form in July, when 20,000 to 30,000 animals gather. Occasionally more than 100,000 gather together, forming the largest animal herds reported outside of Africa. The largest I have seen contained 300,000 caribou.

Perhaps the easiest way to get to know these caribou of the barrens is to follow them through a year of their life. Because of the variable weather, not every year is exactly the same, but there is a general pattern. The description here begins and ends with winter, the longest season by far, a time for perseverance.

DEEP WINTER

In January temperatures are very low and the buildup of snow covers much of the caribou's food supply. Most of the caribou have retreated to the forest, although a few will have taken up residence on bare ridges or mountain slopes where the wind sweeps the ground clear, giving easy access to food but high windchill. Caribou are well equipped to withstand the chill, though. I have seen them on high mountain slopes in Yukon, feeding with their bodies oriented in random directions, seemingly oblivious to the plumes of snow, whipped up by strong gusts, lashing their bodies. The snow swept from these areas trips out where conifers stay the wind's hand, forming drifts near the timberline. In these areas the snow is too deep for caribou to dig through, creating a sort of natural exclosure where caribou cannot feed. A biologist flying over the snow-free winter range in summer can see these patches and compare their lichen load to areas where the caribou could feed.

The caribou in the treed lowlands have almost continuous shelter from the chilling winds, thanks to the ability of conifers to buffer wind speeds that may be 80 kilometres per hour (50 miles per hour) above their crowns but only a breeze at caribou level. For the caribou, being in the trees is almost the equivalent of being in a warm house.

Caribou have several extremely efficient ways of dealing with cold. Their pelage, or hair covering, is designed to meet this need. On the main part of the body the hair is made up of two specialized types. One, the guard hair, is long, somewhat stiff, crimped, hollow and varied in colour. The smaller the body of the individual caribou, the longer the guard hair, since a small body loses heat faster than a larger one. Because the guard hair is stiff, it is not blown around at the whim of the wind and thus warm air stays trapped next to the skin. The crimping creates millions of small air spaces for insulation. The hair is hollow for the same reason. In addition, a hollow core increases the stiffness of the hair without adding weight. The varied colour creates a camouflage, making the caribou less likely to be spotted by its main winter predator, the wolf. This pattern is probably also significant socially, since there are subtle differences in the pattern between the different ages and sexes. The other main type of body hair, the underfur, is more like wool; it is fine, shorter than the guard hair, which protects it, and crimped. Because this hair is fine, it is flexible, allowing it to twist around and between the guard hairs. This underfur acts as goose down does, creating even more insulation.

A caribou's ears also have a very effective combination of long and short, mostly stiff hairs that prevent frostbite to this thinnest part of the body and keep the wind out of it, no matter which way the caribou is facing. Thus, the caribou can continue to feed while the wind swirls. The ear itself is much smaller than that of other members of the deer family because of the cold niche the caribou occupies. This smaller size also makes the ear less vulnerable to frostbite and reduces the surface area through which heat can be lost.

The hair on a caribou's legs and muzzle is short, thick and stiff and is not hollow. Because the hair is short, ice is less likely to form and snow pellets are less likely to build up on it. Short hair is also less likely than long hair to be broken or worn out by the snow, with which the animals are in almost constant contact in this season. In order to feed, the caribou must thrust its muzzle into the snow hundreds of times a day, as well as walking through it almost continuously. If the hair covering of the muzzle became crusted with ice or snow, the caribou's ability

This Svalbard reindeer female and calf, which is in its first winter, are well supplied with the long winter hair necessary to deal with the cold. GEORG BANGJORD

to see, feed and travel would be restricted and it would be vulnerable to predation. Unlike the noses of deer and elk, the caribou nose is furred, like that of moose, to reduce heat loss.

A caribou's legs are cooler than other parts of its body. Cool blood moving from the legs to the body core travels through netted veins that wrap around the warmer arteries, scavenging the heat and thus warming the blood before it enters the body core. The blood in the arteries that pass through the network of veins is precooled, so it loses less heat to the outside. In this way, the caribou avoids fruitlessly heating Arctic air with energy gained at no small effort. What keeps caribou feet from freezing? The answer is that this cooling system is regulated to ensure that enough heat goes to the feet so that even though they are cooled they don't freeze.

Another adaptation to cold is the caribou's specialized nasal passages, where the inner membranes are covered with many fine, short bristles. As the caribou inhales the very cold, dry outside air, it passes over these membranes and cools them. At the same time, the air is heated by the membranes. As the air enters the many tiny sacs in the lungs, it warms further to body temperature and unavoidably absorbs a great deal of vapour from the lung tissue. On exhalation, as the warm moist air passes the cool membranes and bristles of the caribou's nasal passages, much of the water vapour recondenses on them. After several breaths, there is enough water to begin collecting into drops, which then trickle into special folds or gutters tilted towards the back of the nose and throat, where they are swallowed. This recycling of water saves the caribou the heat it would have to use melting ice or snow to replace water that would otherwise be lost to the atmosphere. The short hairs on the end of the caribou's nose further reduce heat loss.

Any one of these small adaptations may not seem like much, but collectively they make the caribou a very efficient beast indeed.

THE WINTER TABLE

Imagine that by some trick you are suddenly transported to the winter range of the Porcupine caribou herd in the forested hills in the watershed of the Ogilvie River in northern Yukon. The average daytime temperature is -35°C (-31°F) in this winter of moderate snowfall. It is February now, and the snow depth is around 50 centimetres (20 inches). You have a camp nearby with a woodstove, so you can always go and stoke up the coals, make some tea and take the chill out of your body.

Now you are out watching a group of these animals, which are amazingly at home in this quite formidable habitat. You are on snowshoes and must move ever so carefully in order to get close to these sometimes weary animals, who are frequently challenged by wolves that must make their living by eating fresh, preferably unfrozen caribou meat. You must get close in order to watch continuously, because using binoculars at this temperature is very hard on the eyes and you can only get glimpses of the action. Moreover, the binoculars tend to frost over in about ten seconds. So you prefer to observe with the naked eye and have developed the skill of instilling trust in the caribou.

There are several groups around made up of females and calves and the odd young male, but rarely mature males. There are other groups of mature males, which sometimes have young males mixed in but no females.

Each animal digs a crater in the snow with a front hoof using a series of quick strokes to move the snow (which is like light, dry sand in such continuous cold).

PAGES 36-37

Caribou of the George River herd run through a winter sunset in northern Quebec.

PATRICE HALLEY

CARIBOU HAVE VERY SENSITIVE

NOSES AND CAN RECOGNIZE THE

SMELL OF LICHEN JUST AS EASILY

AS WE CAN RECOGNIZE

THE SMELL OF ONIONS

COOKING.

These strokes send the snow flying out past the caribou's flank and eventually bare a small piece of ground under its nose, where the caribou can feed on life-giving lichens and other morsels.

The pawing is a lot of work, so the caribou first sniffs the air at the top of the snow for the smell of the food it needs. If that doesn't work, it shoves its snout into the snow to sniff the air in the snow pack. If it smells nothing attractive, it pulls its head out, takes a step or two and shoves it into a different place until it smells the right smell. Caribou have very sensitive noses and can recognize the smell of lichen just as easily as we can recognize the smell of onions cooking. The deeper the snow, the deeper a caribou has to shove its nose into the snow pack to pick up plant odours. It may also have to walk several metres before it finds a spot worth cratering.

If a caribou goes to the trouble of pawing a crater, it usually feeds in it for a few minutes; but sometimes a good crater can occupy one for twenty to thirty minutes. In that case, the caribou usually paws at the edges to enlarge it.

The caribou constantly watch each other as they feed. If one caribou sees that a caribou subordinate to it has found an exceptionally good place to feed, it challenges the subordinate. The subordinate usually doesn't waste energy defending the crater, because it has already had a similar dispute with this individual before and lost. So it walks away, letting the challenger finish off the goodies and hoping to keep its crater a secret longer next time.

Earlier you heard the croak of a raven, which was flying between feeds at the carcass of an old male caribou that the wolves had brought down the night before. The caribou had not recovered from the injuries and exertions of the rut the previous fall and so was weak and made easy prey. The wolves had ended his suffering, feeding themselves and several species of birds, such as ravens, gray jays, boreal chickadees and three-toed woodpeckers, as well as small mammals, including

FACING PAGE

This reindeer in northern
Norway is digging a crater
to feed on lichens and vas-
cular plants hidden from
its eye but not its nose.
MARK AND JULIET YATES/
BBC NHU PICTURE LIBRARY

THE MALES' DOMINANCE DISAPPEARS

WITH THEIR ANTLERS, THOUGH THEY

STILL HAVE DISPUTES, WHICH THEY

SETTLE BY SPARRING,

JABBING AND CLUB-

BING WITH THEIR

FRONT FEET WHILE

STANDING ON THEIR

HIND LEGS.

martens, weasels, hares, deer mice, red-backed voles, brown lemmings and masked shrews. So the ecosystem turns.

After you have watched these wintering caribou for several days and seen many interactions, you begin to see some patterns in caribou behaviour and etiquette. Mature males that did most of the breeding three months earlier largely avoid the female and calf groups at this time of year. They have also lost their antlers. Antlers that towered over everyone during the rut began falling off as soon as the breeding was completed, since they had become a burden to the individual.

The males' dominance disappears with their antlers, though they still have disputes, which they settle by sparring, jabbing and clubbing with their front feet while standing on their hind legs. They still have the largest bodies, but without antlers they are subdominant to animals with antlers. This arrangement makes sense because the female, which still has antlers, must nourish a fetus, and her ability to defend her craters from the mature male benefits her and his offspring. It takes a female a lifetime to produce ten or so calves, whereas a male could feasibly produce that many during one rut. Thus, he is more expendable than the female after he has had a successful rut.

A paradox that becomes evident when you have watched this society for a while is that the young males aged three and four years that are yet to breed have the largest antlers during winter. Are they favoured over the females? No, but they have privileges. They comprise less than 5 per cent of the entire herd, so their nutritional needs are not a great threat to the females. They are important in that they are the future breeders, but they are still learning how to relate to the rest of the herd. If they had no antlers, the big males and antlered females could steal their craters. As future breeders, they are not expendable. The solution is that they carry antlers at this crucial time of year. Their antlers then drop in April, even though it is still two or three months before green-up, when they have made it over the hump of the hardest season. Most nonpregnant females also lose their antlers at this time. The pregnant females are just entering the time of greatest demands from their fetus and have a more urgent need to defend their food sources, so the timing of the antler drop of the others is right to meet these needs, especially if the spring melt is delayed.

Another behaviour you will have noticed is that last spring's calf is still staying close to its mother, who allows her young one to feed in her crater with her or moves to dig another crater for herself when the youngster asks to feed in hers. A calf, being small, is subdominant to any adult. But there seems to be a taboo about stealing a calf's crater. It doesn't seem to matter what the status of a mother is; she will punish any adult, including a large, antlered young male, for stealing her calf's crater by hitting the trespasser with her own antlers.

The only change in the herd's behaviour in spring is that the animals will move to nearby areas that haven't yet been heavily foraged. In some winters, near the end of January, the female groups will start to prefer a northerly direction when they walk to a new site to paw their next crater. During a day they won't seem to have moved much, but over a month a distinct northerly drift will be noticeable. The males don't seem to get the same itch, staying back in the depths of the winter range.

SPRING MIGRATION

There comes a time when the caribou get the urge to really migrate, and after this happens they are definitely on the move, strung out and travelling for hours on end through valleys, over lake ice, along rivers and over mountains. The females need to get to their calving ground, which for all of the large herds in the world is north of their winter range on tundra relatively close to the Arctic Ocean. This more concerted move usually begins sometime in April but can be delayed by deep snow and low energy until the last possible moment, which is mid-May. When migration is delayed, the caribou must move as much as 50 kilometres (30 miles) a day to make it to the calving ground in time. This movement is a spectacular sight, especially when thousands of caribou are involved. When they finally stop to rest, they can become a comical sight. I have seen them lying flat out on their sides, heads on the ground, and all four legs stretched out askew. It looks as if a disaster has struck and killed a whole herd, as the animals lie there totally exhausted. No cud chewing, no heads up—they are just bagged out.

Spring migrations vary from 100 kilometres (60 miles) for herds such as the smallish Central Arctic herd in Alaska to 500 kilometres (300 miles) for the moderately sized Porcupine herd in Eastern Alaska, Yukon and Northwest Territories to 1000 kilometres (600 miles) for parts of the George River herd in Quebec and Labrador; at 700,000, the George River herd is the largest herd in the world. Migration routes vary from year to year, depending on where the animals

FACING PAGE

Ice heaved by some of the

highest tides in the world

presents a dangerous obstacle

to these caribou in spring

migration along Quebec's

Arctic coastline.

MIKE BEEDELL/CANADA

IN STOCK/IVY IMAGES

wintered and therefore where the starting point is. The routes lead to terrain that makes the journey fairly easy, such as north-oriented ridges or frozen lakes, but also to barriers such as canyons or huge, raging rivers, which the caribou must go around or cross.

I have followed many spring migration trails and seen some remarkable routes taken. Once I watched several thousand caribou travelling along the bottom of a wide north-south valley containing a lone 600-metre (2,000-foot) mountain. The migrating caribou had the choice of going around either side of this obstacle on flat ground, but they didn't see it as an obstacle at all. They wanted either a change of scenery or a chance to look around for navigational purposes, because they all climbed to the summit and then went down the other side and continued along the valley.

These animals are like Olympic marathon athletes as they relentlessly pursue their course, but certain barriers will stop them. Deep, soft snow will halt them (they may even have to go back a bit to find food), and they must wait for it to melt before moving on. If the snow is deep and crusted, they can travel on top during the night and early morning. The snow softens as the day warms, stopping them in their tracks until it hardens again.

Rivers can present barriers as well. Caribou are very proficient swimmers, but rivers in flood running bank to bank with swirling ice pans, rapids with huge, standing waves, or precipitous falls can take their toll—although not always. One year I was camped along the Porcupine River above Old Crow, Yukon, with two Native helpers, waiting for the spring migration of the Porcupine herd to arrive. We needed to do counts to determine how many of the previous year's calves had reached yearling status. No caribou had yet arrived and we were enjoying a warm, leisurely afternoon when, with a boom, the ice began to go out of the river. The rest of the afternoon the air was full of the roar of ice pans grating on ice pans. The ground shook with ice grinding against the shore and river bottom. It was hard to sleep that night beside such a thundering torrent.

When we woke next morning, things had quieted down as the densely packed ice jam had swept by. The succeeding ice pans were separated by spaces full of slush and so were quieter as they flowed past, though when one hit shore or a bar it slowed down or swung in the current, causing several violent collisions in chain reaction. About midday the migration arrived, and many groups of caribou started plunging into a river that was still wall-to-wall moving ice. But they swam through the slush between the pans and climbed out the other side. I feared for them, expecting that any moment several caribou would be smashed between two colliding pans, but I never saw it happen. Occasionally a group would climb up onto a pan and stand there as it floated down the river out of sight.

Parts of the home ranges for most caribou herds are laced with hundreds, if not thousands, of lakes and rivers, large and small. To use their range efficiently, caribou are equally at home on land and in water. They will swim across a lake as willingly as they will walk around it. Rivers require an assessment of their danger—not necessarily of what is in front of the animal but of what is in the path that the running water will sweep them along. Initially I wasn't sure that caribou could make this assessment.

PAGES 46–47
*The water is shallow
enough here for the caribou
to plunge along rather than
swim, a travel mode they
also use in deep snow.*
MICHIO HOSHINO/
MINDEN PICTURES

During one spring migration of the Porcupine caribou herd a huge blizzard in late May dumped a half-metre (a couple of feet) of snow over all of northern Yukon. By the end of May, just a few days before calving was to begin, the caribou were in the upper parts of the Firth River drainage, still 80 kilometres (50 miles) south of their destination. On May 30 and 31 there was a heat wave, all that fresh snow was turning to liquid at once, and I saw, from our survey plane, phenomena that I never knew could occur, such as slush avalanches coursing down mountain slopes and gullies and sloshing far up the sides of the gullies as they rushed around bends.

This thaw was dumping huge quantities of water into the Firth, which was higher than I'd ever seen it. It was also very wide, and there were 3-metre (10-foot) standing waves right where the caribou had been crossing before it was in flood. When I saw this torrent my heart leapt into my throat because I believed the migrants would be jumping in to cross the river anyway. I could imagine them being ground up and spit out by this raging beast of a river.

But the tracks in the snow told a different story. The trail diverted to parallel the river. I thought, "Well, they will eventually get frustrated and jump in farther down." But no. From the air I followed their trails, which went up and down over many high ridges and mountains. The caribou travelled to the coastal plain this way and successfully crossed the river where it split into many less dangerous channels on its delta fan. They continued on to the western part of the calving range in Alaska, arriving in the nick of time. They would soon be "dropping their calves," a misnomer, since they normally lie down during their short labour and don't "drop" the calves at all.

I was heartened to find that I had been wrong in my assessment of the caribou's intelligence. Sometimes these animals will take stock of a dangerous situation and change routes to steer clear of disaster. At other times, however, they don't see the danger, as at Limestone Falls in northern Quebec, when ten thousand George River herd animals died in 1984 crossing the Caniapiscau River in a flood. But more often than not, I now believe, caribou do avert potential tragedy by intelligently assessing dangerous situations.

One might wonder why, just as the weather starts to improve on the wintering ground, the females get it into their heads that they must go to the harsher climate of the Arctic tundra to give birth. In fact, they are giving their youngsters a treat, for caribou like cool and what comes with it—even the calves. Rather than make the calves trek north after they are born, the mothers do them the service of carrying them there in a belly pack. Next to the still-frozen Arctic Ocean, harassment from biting insects is delayed at least a month after these insects appear at the wintering grounds farther south. Biting insects are hardest on calves, with their short hair.

The first rapid growth of high-quality forage is similarly delayed, but the timing is just right for the nutritional needs of both calf and adult. The move also occurs just as most wolves become tied to a den site. Most wolves on the winter range or migration path stay put; only a few migrate with or ahead of the caribou. Thus, going north is an anti-predator strategy as well. Through a combination of factors, the Arctic tundra is the place to be for giving birth.

The first arrivals normally travel to the far end of the calving ground to make room for the caribou behind. They may just barely get onto the tundra when they are faced with deep, wind-packed, continuous snow cover on the route they would normally take. It is too hard to dig through this snow. If they cannot see or smell bare ground beyond this obstacle, they will stop and wait for the strong sun to melt it before going on. If the caribou behind them were to continue along the migration trail, there would soon be wall-to-wall caribou on a tiny patch of tundra, and trampling would destroy the plant cover, causing permafrost to melt and soil to erode later. To avoid this circumstance, the pregnant females seem to develop a prickliness at this time of year and maintain large distances between themselves. Thus, when the lead caribou stop, the caribou behind them stop wherever they are and all feed or rest. The need to stop is telegraphed all the way back along the migration route to the last group. The caribou don't go on until they see no bums ahead. Only then do they move on until they catch up, stopping again if those ahead have also stopped. In this way they move onto the calving ground during years of delayed snowmelt.

RATHER THAN MAKE THE CALVES TREK NORTH AFTER THEY ARE BORN, THE MOTHERS DO THEM THE SERVICE OF CARRYING THEM THERE IN A BELLY PACK.

CALVING TIME

As the females move onto the calving ground, they are accompanied by their previous year's female calves, now yearlings, which are becoming familiar with the migration routes and the calving ground itself. Most male yearlings have left their mothers to learn about the later timing and spring migration routes of the males and the range they use during the calving period. This range is often adjacent to the calving ground proper but never on it. The females spread themselves out evenly over the most available parts of their area, according to where the snow has melted. Different parts melt off at different times, depending on the snow pack and the persistence of the cloud cover or fog. Through much of the calving period the caribou feed on sedges, especially the flower buds of the cotton grass sedge, and freshened lichens. Little else has started to grow yet.

As the days approach when almost all of the calves will be born (between June 5 and 12 for the Western Arctic, Porcupine, Bluenose, Bathhurst, Beverly and Qamanirjuaq herds, and between June 12 and 20 for the George and Leaf River herds), the females spread out over a huge area to drop their calves. The size of the area varies with the size of the herd, ranging from 5,000 to 30,000 square kilometres (2,000 to 12,000 square miles). Spreading out is good anti-predator strategy, since it guarantees that the calves will be scattered thinly during their most vulnerable time, the first week after they are born. If they were concentrated, predators could kill many calves in a short time. The spacing also provides a large

FACING PAGE

A very young caribou enjoying some rare sunshine and dry conditions in June, when the Arctic is often overcast, foggy and damp.

FRED BRUEMMER

DURING THE FIRST

WEEK OR TWO OF

ITS LIFE, THE CALF

SLEEPS 70 TO

80 PER CENT OF

THE TIME.

area near the birth site for each female to feed on during this crucial time when her calf needs to sleep and grow. The synchronicity of the calving is also good anti-predator strategy, since it is all over before the predators have had time to take full advantage of it.

During the birthing time, if you look out over a large area, you will see many caribou lying down flat on their sides. Sometimes a head comes up a little. You can see the caribou wriggling and squirming in a way that looks as if they are slightly uncomfortable. This behaviour usually lasts at most a few hours. Then the new mother is up on her feet, head down, licking at the new arrival to invigorate it and dry it off. The calf is soon up on its feet looking for its first meal. Its legs are wobbly for a few minutes before it finds the right location for snack time, and then the calf lies down to rest before trying it all over again. It is hard for this wee one to move around for the first three days because its legs are very long, like those of a colt, and its hind legs are bent forward under its belly, causing it to lose its balance easily and fall down. The bend is exaggerated on the calf's first day but not so much on its second and third days, and it is nearly straight by the fourth day.

Soon a routine develops in which the calf sleeps and the mother feeds; then the tiny tawny calf gets up and nurses for five to fifteen minutes and maybe plays a bit by itself or with a neighbour calf. It will run or buck in small circles near its mother, or it may playfully paw at some snow, already practising what it will have to do millions of times each winter of its life. With a neighbour it may race or sniff or rear and play-box with its front feet—more practice for future activities. The play soon ends, and the calf lies down for another nap. During the first week or two of its life, the calf sleeps 70 to 80 per cent of the time. By the sixth or seventh day it can run as fast as or faster than its mother, if she has fed relatively well during the winter and was thus able to fully nourish the calf as a fetus, and if she has an ample supply of milk. The calf has now passed the time when it was most vulnerable to predators,

FACING PAGE

Fortunately, this Alaskan calf's mother has had a good winter, indicated by her straight back and smooth sides—no ribs show. With the bare ground and thick vegetation, the mother should have a good milk supply and the calf will likely have good speed if challenged by predators.
S.J. KRASEMANN/PETER ARNOLD, INC.

although after a winter of deep snow and a late spring, the calf may not have received adequate nutrition and may continue to be vulnerable through the summer.

Usually at calving time the mother is still wearing the hard antlers she has used all winter in her social interactions and in defence against wolves. About a week after the birth these antlers become loose and annoying as she moves her head to feed. When they are properly loose, she bends her neck to place her head near her flank and kicks her antlers off with a hind foot, sending them cartwheeling across the tundra. She has retained these weapons until the calf is fast on its feet, but no longer. Sometimes the antlers just fall off when they are loose enough.

The antler drop deposits calcium on the calving ground. After the female drops her antlers, they are slowly eaten by arctic hare and rodents, whose decomposing droppings release calcium into the soil. The calcium is then taken up by plants that the female eats, thus guaranteeing that it will be available to make milk and help form the bones of the new calves. Females also chew directly on the old, shed antlers. If caribou relied on the breakdown of rock and movement of calcium through the permafrost, or if the calving ground were on calcium-poor rock, they would run short. The female grows most of her antlers during August and September, well away from the calving ground, so they are made with minerals from other parts of the range. This mineral recycling system allows a population to have a specific and fixed calving ground.

The normal weather during calving can be described in one word: "clammy." The weather can range from snow to strong, cold winds to fog to rain to grey overcast skies, day after clammy day. It is a tough test of a calf's ability to maintain its body warmth. Swirling storm systems pound away at the Arctic as warm air tries to invade the domain of Superjack Frost. Front after front causes collisions of air masses, generally keeping things miserable while the backbone of winter is finally broken, albeit for a desperately short time.

FACING PAGE

Two calves pause in an Alaskan mountain tundra valley while playing together, an activity that strengthens their growing bones and muscles.

KIM HEACOX/PETER ARNOLD, INC.

While calving is going on, many of the yearling females seem to lose patience with their mothers, who have had to become sedentary for the sake of their newborns. The yearlings and the few barren females, not being tied down, still have the wanderlust. They form small bands and wander about at a faster pace. These groups are amusing to watch and are reminiscent of teenage gangs going about looking for excitement, if not trouble.

After the calves become mobile, the females and their charges form groups called nursery bands. At first these bands are slower moving than the adolescent gangs because the calves are still slow and want to sleep often. Around the time of the summer solstice, more green plants appear on the birthing range and the calves become stronger and larger, have less need for sleep and can travel faster. The two types of bands start to merge. Thus starts the process of aggregation, which continues in a big way after the solstice.

FACING PAGE
Young adult caribou of the international Porcupine herd. ART WOLFE

PAGES 58-59
Porcupine caribou cross the Kongakut River as they head east towards Yukon along the Alaskan coastal plain in the Arctic National Wildlife Refuge, a part of their calving ground. The area has been protected since 1960 but is now being threatened by oil companies that want to drill and build pipelines. KIM HEACOX/ PETER ARNOLD, INC.

A TIME OF GREEN, A TIME TO GATHER

By summer solstice, air temperatures have risen to the point that plants can grow rapidly with twenty-four hours of daylight. Clear and sunny skies are most common in July. The tundra suddenly turns very green, especially where there is shrubbery or relatively tall herbaceous plants, such as near the margins of lakes and streams. The caribou often start their annual molt at this time. The males usually start this procedure earlier than the females, whose physiology is more stressed by the previous eight months of gestation and nursing a calf. The first hair to shed is on the eyelids, followed by hair on the nose and face. Then large patches of new hair start to appear in somewhat unpredictable places. The result is that for much of July many caribou are pinto patterned, the old hair bleached almost white and the new hair black. In good years many of the bulls are totally black by early July; a large portion of the females turn black a week or more later. Soon after that, as the hair continues to grow, they become chocolate coloured.

The males have also been growing large antlers, covered by light to dark brown velvet, since May. By now the new antlers are full sized; only the tips have to form. As mineral continues to be deposited throughout the antlers, they increase in density and strength. The females have just started to grow their antlers, which look like short, blunt, rounded Ts growing close to their heads.

The calves are at least twice the weight they were at birth and are soon to be weaned off a rich supply of milk. Some of them start to molt, changing from a

FACING PAGE

A large post-calving aggregation of the Quebec and Labrador George River herd swims across a river during its midsummer travels over the tundra.

PATRICE HALLEY

tawny colour to dark brown, first on the back and then on the remainder of the body. They still have very long legs and, if well nourished, can run like the wind.

The fast greening of the tundra initiates the most spectacular behaviour of these caribou. They lose the prickliness they had during calving and take on the opposite characteristic—cohesiveness. As bands encounter each other on the calving ground and begin to travel out onto the rest of the tundra as well, they merge and move on together. This process continues, with far more merging than splitting of groups. The result is that quite quickly there are huge groups surging along unpredictable routes. They travel very fast at this time, most days moving 15 to 25 kilometres (10 to 15 miles), often upwind, making it harder for mosquitoes to pester them.

These large groups are called post-calving aggregations. They form every year but are more noticeable in years when the population of biting insects is high. The larger and tighter a group is when the insects are very active, the fewer bites the animals get, simply because there are fewer bugs per caribou on a given piece of ground. These bad bug days are warm, calm days. If the weather in July is cool and windy, the insects have to drop to the ground and cling to the vegetation to avoid getting blown away. During such times the caribou can spread out, relax and tank up on food, though they still travel a substantial distance in a day. For this reason, aggregations of caribou are not as tightly gathered together and therefore are not as apparent in years when the weather is cool and windy.

Two or three parts of the summer range may be used, with several groups in each part. These areas can be hundreds of kilometres apart, as they are for the George River herd, to only 50 kilometres (30 miles) apart for the Bluenose herd. The groups will remain distinct, sometimes for the duration of the aggregation period. The caribou are still feeding on sedge leaves early in the month, but the leaves soon become quite indigestible and the animals switch to flowering plants and birch and willow leaves.

I HAVE SEEN MANY NATURAL

SPECTACLES, BUT THE SIGHT OF A

HUGE AGGREGATION OF CARIBOU IS

ONE OF THE MOST

AWE-INSPIRING IN

NORTH AMERICA.

I have seen many natural spectacles, but the sight of a huge aggregation of caribou is one of the most awe-inspiring in North America. Even seeing a group of only 20,000 or 30,000 caribou is a very emotional experience. The largest group I have seen consisted of over 300,000 caribou. I am confident of this last number because after it broke into six, more manageable, groups I helped photograph and count them. Forty-two radio-collared caribou that were in the original group helped us keep track of where each splinter group travelled. This group, and a group of 160,000 caribou that I photographed and counted in another year, were part of the George River herd. A census team I was part of years earlier saw a group of 100,000 caribou comprising 90 per cent of the Porcupine herd. Until then none of us had ever knowingly seen such a large group. It was the culmination of an amazing five days—five days that taught me how fast caribou can aggregate.

On June 29 most females in the population were scattered out deep into the northern foothills of the Brooks Range in Alaska. As we flew over them that evening, they were all on the march north towards the Arctic coastal plain. The next day all of the caribou had left the foothills and were on the southern edge of the plain. By July 2 they were all next to the coast. On the fourth of July they had moved east to the Yukon border and were in one group of 100,000 on the edge of Demarcation Bay. In only five days they had moved from being widely scattered inside the Brooks Range into one group covering at the most 20 square kilometres (8 square miles).

One could ask how these caribou simultaneously, as though they were one organism, began coalescing in such a coordinated fashion. Is such an aggregation a purely instinctual response to a stimulus? Or is it a more conscious decision, or even the result of an unrecognized intelligence? The generally accepted explanation is that it is the result of insect harassment, yet these aggregations sometimes occur

PAGES 64-65
A large aggregation travels over an Arctic plain. Polygons formed by ice lenses lie in a honeycomb shape under the surface of the tundra.
MICHIO HOSHINO/
MINDEN PICTURES

when the insects are not on the wing. In the case just described, there were light snow squalls on June 29, when it all began. But I have also observed such large gatherings when it was warm and received hardly a bite from mosquitoes. These may be exceptional incidents, but they show that insects are not the only stimulus causing the caribou to gather in July.

A more important question to be asked is why the caribou form these huge groups in July only, and not at any other time of the year. Again, the commonly accepted answer is that the insects are the worst at that time of year. I studied the George River herd during the summer for six consecutive years. During this time the caribou displayed another behaviour that shines new light on this subject. The post-calving aggregations never used the same ground in the summer range until the sixth summer. This observation suggests that they were following a natural rest/rotation grazing regime, with a five-year rest period for each portion of the summer range.

It is in July that the new plant growth of the year is occurring at its fastest. As ranchers know, forage plants are most vulnerable to grazing at this time. The process I have just described leaves most of the summer range untouched for five years after being grazed at this sensitive time.

Part of the process may include light grazing as well. Studies have found that some caribou, especially females, may lose weight during July. Some herds also have a high adult mortality rate in July. This may result from heat stress in this cold-adapted animal. It could also be the result of stress from the animals' high output of energy as they travel or possibly a low intake of nutrients.

FACING PAGE

A large bull confidently plunges into the deep, fast water of an Alaskan river. TOM WALKER

Large groups also serve as an anti-predator tactic. With 99 per cent of the summer range devoid of caribou, wolves have to travel farther to make a kill. The herd is also thought to provide a sense of security to each individual within the group, with so many other nearby group members for the wolves to prey upon. This strategy is called swamping the predators.

When you are near one of these large gatherings, it is an auditory experience as well as a splendid visual one. There are the clicks of many ankles as the caribou speed along and the vocalizations of calves and mothers to each other. Sometimes the males tune in with their hoots too. Calves make a loud belching sound when they get nervous or are trying to reconnect with their mothers within the herd. The mother's call can be loud, like the calf's, or a quieter grunting sound.

If a lost calf doesn't locate its mother by calling, it stops and is left behind. But the mother too drops back. If they both have stopped at the same time, they see each other. If they drop out at different times, however, the reunion is not so easy, and they trot back and forth along the back trail of the herd for several kilometres until they find each other. These animals use this very effective alternative behaviour that turns confusion into simplicity when the latter is needed. Most social species that form large groups, such as wildebeest and cattle, use this method to reunite mother-young pairs.

FACING PAGE

A fast-moving post-calving aggregation of the Porcupine herd in Alaska. MICHIO HOSHINO/MINDEN PICTURES

AUGUST: A TIME TO SCATTER

Meanwhile, the wolves have been trying to keep their pups fed through June and July while most of the caribou are far to the north. As the caribou scatter in August, they start to move back towards the wolves, who challenge them more often. In years that young and old caribou have been weakened by unfavourable weather during the previous winter, mortality is high. Good years for the caribou can mean not-so-good years for the wolves, who can find only a few old and sick animals they can outrun. In such years it may be the wolf pups that don't make it instead of caribou calves, and under these conditions the caribou population is stable and growing while the wolf population is stable or falling.

At the other end of the cycle the caribou numbers may have increased to the point that their range has started to suffer. Poor range supports fewer strong caribou. Fewer strong caribou calves and adults mean that more pups survive and the wolves start reversing the population trend in the caribou.

As the range comes into full growth, the caribou start to spread out and feed more concertedly. They will stay longer in an area before moving to another attractive site. If you are on the range at this time of year, you will find it is a tranquil time, with sunny, windy or wet days. Sometimes you may have it all in one day if a squall moves through. If you climb up on a hill, your first impression will probably be that the countryside is completely devoid of life, but if you sit down and slowly study the landscape with binoculars you will likely find a few chocolate-coloured caribou feeding,

It is fattening and resting time for this mature male as he readies himself for the chance of his lifetime, the rut, when he would only be caught dead in this position.
MARTIN W. GROSNICK

lying down or just standing there. They will be singletons, female-calf pairs or even small groups. Contrasted with the frenetic times of July, this sublime moment seems like a dream. Yet it goes on for much of August and September. The caribou fatten rapidly and the calves grow to at least half the height of the adults, more in good years.

By September the caribou begin to develop a white mane and a white horizontal slash across the lower body. This pattern provides camouflage in snow. In the west, the barren-ground caribou develop a dark body colour at this time, while the woodland caribou of the George River herd in the east can vary from quite dark to a light tan. Their legs are tan to grey and their feet are white. The muzzle can be tan to grey to dark brown, while the rump has a white patch with a white tail.

Now the males get ready for breeding season. The velvet begins to shred and fall off their antlers, turning them crimson red with blood. As the males slash at shrubs and trees, however, the antler colour changes from red to a light or dark brown. With huge antlers and swelling neck, as his body prepares for the combat that will soon occur, the male is a magnificent sight. His behaviour changes, and he begins having mild sparring matches with other males to exercise his growing muscles. The females watch with what seems to be amusement, but their witnessing this buildup of male aggression helps synchronize the onset of estrus, which later helps them calve within days of each other and hence coordinate the early stages of calf growth.

The females are splendid in their own right. Their antlers have grown considerably by now but will remain in velvet into October. About 1 per cent of females never grow antlers. The antlerless gene these females carry illustrates the caribou's varying genetic makeup.

The calves too are getting dressed up. Some of them have even grown little spikes for antlers.

FACING PAGE

This Alaskan caribou bull is just beginning to shed his velvet. MARTIN W. GROSNICK

FACING PAGE

A Denali herd bull stains
and shines up his antlers in
preparation for the mating
season. JOE MCDONALD

As September progresses the caribou begin to travel a bit more, and unmixed groups of males or females merge so that all can participate in the mating season. The caribou will likely still be in their late summer range when the first snowstorm hits. If it is a serious snowfall, it will initiate the fall migration towards the winter range. When the snow lets up the migration usually slows or stops and much of the snow may even melt, but it has set the tone, and a trend towards the winter range is in effect. Ice begins forming on the lakes, and by mid-October the caribou can usually walk on them.

As the first half of October passes, snow is more persistent, pushing the caribou on towards their winter domain. All the caribou are at their fattest at this point, since they have had access to food rich in nutrients. The leaves have largely fallen off the deciduous shrubs and larch trees. With their contrasting coats, the caribou are quite visible against the dark, wet vegetation as they slowly trek south, west or east.

*A barren-ground caribou bull
about to enter the rutting
season very fat and dressed to
the nines. He even seems to
have painted a curtain of
aurora borealis on his side.*
MICHAEL S. QUINTON

PAGES 78–79
*Two large males spar in
Denali National Park as
they strengthen their swelling
neck muscles in preparation
for the rut, when serious
fights may break out. The
bull on the right still has
blood from his recently shed
velvet near the base of his
antlers.* KIM HEACOX/
PETER ARNOLD, INC.

THE RUT: A TIME FOR RUNNING

By now the caribou are in full regalia. Their pelage patterns are fully developed, and the males' gigantic antlers, stained and polished for display, are sharply pointed and tower far above their backs. Their necks are bulked up for serious combat. The females' antlers are fully formed, though they may not have shed their velvet yet, and their coats too are in fine finish. To behold a caribou in full dress during the rut, or mating season, is exhilarating. The caribou must enjoy the visual effect of this dress-up time as well.

When the mating season arrives, excitement reigns as males begin to have serious fights. They also start chasing females, sometimes at quite high speeds. The larger the group, the more chaotic the behaviour appears and sounds, with males hooting defiantly at each other and antlers crashing as others engage in sparring matches.

At this time there can be large and small groups. The larger groups can consist of two hundred to five thousand animals, depending on the size of the population, and the smaller groups contain five to thirty animals. The smaller groups are often quite sedentary, whereas the larger groups usually move very fast, streaming over the fall migration route at a hectic pace, sometimes covering several hundred kilometres during the rut. They may spontaneously change or even reverse their direction of travel, altering the progress of the fall migration for as much as a third to a half of the population and thus influencing where they winter.

THROUGH CONTINUOUS COURTSHIP,

URINE TASTING AND FREQUENT

ATTEMPTS TO MOUNT, A TENDING

MALE DISCOVERS

WHEN THE FEMALE

IS READY TO MATE.

As the hectic pace is maintained, the mating goes on, with most of the females entering estrus within a week to ten days of each other and the largest males fighting for the right to tend females, or guard them as they approach estrus. The losing males race about looking for other prospective females and chasing younger males away from females. Through continuous courtship, urine tasting and frequent attempts to mount, a tending male discovers when the female is ready to mate. The actual coitus is so brief that an observer could miss it by blinking. The breeding males expend an enormous amount of energy. By the time the rut ends, about two weeks after it has started, they are no longer round and fat but have the gaunt shape of a greyhound. The females normally breed just once, reserving their energy for the gestation period, which normally lasts 225 to 235 days.

In a population with a healthy range, most of the males will take part in the rut and most females will be bred within a two-week period. The few females that do not breed may cycle again in three weeks. But producing such late-arriving calves does not bode well for their survival. When the range is hurting, as was the range of the George River herd during the nineties, the sexes may be so scattered that they don't mix properly before the rut and most of the males may not even be present for the mating season. Given this and the poorer condition of females, relatively few will calve the next spring.

The normal age for females to mature is 1½ or 2½ years, and they breed most of the following years, barring accidents. Once in a while a population is poised for an extremely high growth rate because it is colonizing a new range or is recovering from a long period of low productivity, which has depressed numbers on a traditional range. At such a time the calves will grow so large and healthy that the females experience estrus in their first fall, when they are a mere 5 months old, meaning that they will give birth when they are yearlings. This phenomenon is very unusual, but it is a mechanism built into the species that allows the caribou to take advantage of unusually high

FACING PAGE

A reluctant female reindeer dodges the advances of a male by twisting out from under him. LAURIE CAMPBELL

productive periods in their range. In very unproductive times the young females will experience delayed puberty and not produce calves until they are 4 or 5 years old.

At the tail end of the rut the young males are still interested, even though the females are mostly bred. Unlike the big males, the young males have remained in good condition because, with a glance at them during the main breeding season, the large males made these subordinates drop their heads and feed, sublimating their sexual behaviour. As the large males lose interest, they are no longer there to inhibit the young males, who suddenly become more active. Their courting may continue through the winter in a mild way, especially in easy winters.

FACING PAGE

This bull adds some calcium to his diet as he chews on an old shed antler. STEVE KAUFMAN

LATE FALL TO EARLY WINTER

As the rut draws to a close, antlers start falling off the large males, which have just done most of the breeding. It is a sad sight when the first of the magnificent males appears with only one antler. It's almost as if he has been injured, but it is the beginning of the natural progression into the nonbreeding season.

As the rut peters out, the caribou continue towards the winter range. Their new pelage, acquired just a few weeks ago, is essential now that the severe cold season is about to arrive. There may be no snow or as much as 40 to 50 centimetres (16 to 20 inches), though on average it would be less than half of that. This depth is easy to travel through and feed in. The caribou can use very short, quick paw strokes to obtain grasses, sedges, shrubs, dried flowering plant stems and lichen.

As darkness takes over in November, the snow builds and soon winter begins. The caribou diet has changed to three-quarters lichen from only one-quarter during summer. The sexes begin a process of segregation as the antlerless males start preferring their own company, for several reasons. They are less sensitive to danger than females, who still have their calves at heel and an embryo to protect and nourish, causing them to be very conservative. The mature males, with little need to conserve energy, often travel to the outer fringes of the winter range and even into areas that haven't been visited for years. If this range has sufficiently recovered since the last time it was used, the females may follow them later that winter or in succeeding winters.

IT IS A SAD SIGHT

WHEN THE FIRST OF

THE MAGNIFICENT

MALES APPEARS WITH

ONLY ONE ANTLER.

A bull looks or sniffs
for food in a large crater.
MARTIN W. GROSNICK

The winter range, where lichen grows in thick mats 10 centimetres (4 inches) deep, is largely untouched by caribou during the dry summer season. When dry, these plants are very brittle and vulnerable to trampling. If you ignite them, they burst into flame almost like gasoline, illustrating that they are packed with calories and therefore vital to caribou in winter. When the lichens are damp, they are much less vulnerable to damage when they are stepped on. They grow at most a half-centimetre (quarter-inch) per summer, so it takes many years for a heavily used portion of winter range to recover. Although high in carbohydrates, lichens are low in protein. Caribou compensate for their low nitrogen intake in winter by recycling protein in the form of urea in their saliva. They may also do so through their blood.

PREDATION

After being around caribou for many years, when I imagine them now, somewhere in or near that image saunters a wolf. That is because a healthy caribou population is one with a healthy range, and wolves are sensitive to caribou range condition. Some wolves will suffer and starve when the range is good; they get fat and have lots of pups when that range goes down in quality. This is not to say that other predators are unnecessary, only that wolves are the most important predator, given their size, speed of reproduction and method of killing. Grizzly and black bears den for at least half the year, and when they come out they eat plants and often prefer to scavenge winter kills and wolf kills rather than make their own kills. The only dedicated predator of caribou is the wolf, which does not go vegetarian on them and follows them throughout the year wherever they go. Even if some packs may stop to den up and have their pups far away from the summer range, a few wolves manage to be there as unattached wanderers or as packs that travel to and den on the calving ground several weeks ahead of their prey.

I first saw wolf responses to range in the Porcupine herd. In the late sixties a biologist in Alaska estimated that the herd contained 160,000 caribou. I started studying it in 1971. For at least three winters in a row, the snow was unusually deep. As a result, the caribou females were very skinny in early spring when they were migrating. During the summers, when trailing a large group of caribou, we would stumble upon wolf-killed carcasses of calves and adults on the tundra.

FACING PAGE

A domestic reindeer herd in northern Sweden rests comfortably on lake ice. The semidarkness is typical of subarctic winter days. The ice fog indicates that the air temperature is at least -25°C (-10°F). BENGT LUNDBERG/ BBC NHU PICTURE LIBRARY

THE ONLY DEDICATED PREDATOR

OF CARIBOU IS THE WOLF, WHICH

DOES NOT GO VEGETARIAN ON THEM

AND FOLLOWS THEM

THROUGHOUT THE

YEAR WHEREVER

THEY GO.

We also saw several kills take place. Calf survival through each summer was low. Wolves were plentiful, and several dens were located in the summer range.

In 1977 almost all the wolves died of rabies. By that time, the caribou herd had been reduced to 70,000. In the meantime winter snow accumulations had decreased to 60 centimetres (2 feet) from over 1 metre (3 feet) earlier in the decade. Because the snow was shallower, females travelled to the calving ground in good condition and had strong calves, most of which survived, meaning that the wolves had a rough time catching them. We found no calf mortality during such summers. In 1979 I photographed all the caribou in the herd and counted 113,000. By 1985 they were estimated at 180,000. Numbers can change fast as conditions change for both predator and prey.

The George River herd could well be an example of what happens when the wolves are not protected on a herd's summer range. This herd started to increase in number in the 1960s and continued to do so into the 1990s, to the point of damaging its summer range, which had more than a half-million caribou feeding on it by then. Normally wolves would respond by becoming extremely numerous on this summer range. This has not happened. To help this herd recover to more balanced numbers, perhaps the hunters and managers should protect the wolf on its summer range. Humans usually cannot replace the most efficient predator of a species, which for the caribou is the wolf. The wolf is their greatest ally in ensuring a future with wild caribou meat in it for the hunters of the North and their families. For their health and spirit, there can be no better future.

Without wolves on the summer range to reduce an overabundant herd and prevent it from damaging its summer range, a herd seems to limp along for a while, continuing to damage its range. Ultimately many caribou will starve and the range will then take longer to recover. Then it will take longer for the caribou to return to abundant numbers again.

FACING PAGE
A gray wolf runs through snow with little trouble. DANIEL J. COX/NATURAL EXPOSURES

PAGES 90–91
A reindeer bull grazes in the sunset. LAURIE CAMPBELL

CARIBOU
Part Three
AND NORTHERN
PEOPLE

THE CARIBOU IN MYTH AND LEGEND

According to an Inuit creation myth, first there was a man and a woman before there were any other creatures. The woman dug a hole in the ground and began fishing. One by one she pulled up the animals, the last being Tuktu, the caribou. The creator was well pleased and told the woman that the caribou would be the most important animal for the people to hunt. The woman sent the caribou out to fill the land with many caribou.

After a time, the land was filled with caribou, and the woman's sons went out and hunted them. Since they killed only the large, strong caribou, the family ate well. But eventually there were more small, weak caribou than large, strong ones. The sons became worried and told the woman of their concern. She used her magic to complain to the Creator, saying that his work was no good, for there were too many weak and small caribou. If her people ate them, they would become weak and sick too. The Creator answered, saying that on the contrary, his work was good, and he would tell Amorak, the wolf, to go out and hunt the weak caribou. After this, the land was left mainly for the large and fat caribou. This is why, to this day, the caribou and the wolf are one; the caribou feeds the wolf, and the wolf keeps the caribou strong.

This myth encapsulates scientists' conclusions about the wolf–caribou–human hunter partnership in most of the northern ecosystems, described in Part 2. If the relationship is working well, the caribou usually are not depleted and they then do

FACING PAGE

*Caribou have traditionally
played an important role
in northern cultures.*
THOMAS MANGELSEN/
IMAGES OF NATURE

not deplete their range and become scarce for decades while the range recovers. Caribou are, and traditionally were, an extremely important component in the culture of northern people. Just as cattle are a major source of protein in the south, so caribou are the main source of protein in northern cultures. But caribou meat contains twice as much protein as beef and much less saturated fat. Even though they are half the size of a steer or even smaller, caribou supply as much protein and more healthful, unsaturated fats to the diet. It seems paradoxical that animals living in a land of such scarcity could themselves be so full of nutrition, but it is true. They also supply northern cultures with a great deal of spiritual nourishment.

While studying caribou, I lived in villages of predominantly Inuit, Dene or Cree people. Although making flying surveys and working up data took a lot of my time and energy, I had the opportunity to talk to people about their experiences with and ideas about caribou. They told me stories about their own history, their ancestors and their methods for surviving under such harsh conditions.

People told me that in the past what they called medicine was an important part of their existence. Only shamans had full medicine, which enabled them to obtain the cooperation of one or more animal spirits, who worked on behalf of the shamans. Half medicine, which most people had, allowed them to know where and when it was best to hunt and also to know about coming events before they happened, even though they might be kilometres from the nearest source of such knowledge. For example, the late Big Joe Kay of Old Crow was resting in a remote hunting camp when he felt a tugging at his sleeve and heard his sister's voice saying, "Hurry up! Why are you taking so long?" He was a superb athlete and ran 100 kilometres (60 miles) to the village. He arrived there an hour before his sister died.

Hunters often had hunches about where to search for their prey. They could not abuse this gift and had to show great respect to any animal they killed (they understood that the animal had given its body to the hunter and his associates).

Through rituals and taboos, hunters showed the animal that they held no malice towards it but simply needed to eat. The Inuit did this by leaving gifts of small carvings on the ground, on the ice or in the water, depending on where they killed the animal. They also observed a taboo against mixing types of meat. The Inuit never stored the meat of caribou and seal together and never ate them in the same meal. The Dene never ate caribou and fish together for the same reason. There was also a very strong taboo against wasting any of the useful resources the animal's body supplied. There were right ways to do things and there were wrong ways. Such observations of respect gave order to people's lives and gave them a way to feel good about themselves in a contradictory world where they had to eat the animals they identified with so much.

Many of the people's stories are of privation. To hear or read these stories, one would think that people were often starving. But normally they had plenty to eat. When food was scarce, however, people starved to death, leaving a strong memory. It was important to talk about these times, both for therapeutic reasons and to remember the mistakes that were made so that they could be averted in the future. To lose family, friends and a support system was devastating physically and emotionally, as well as socially, and needed to be avoided if at all possible.

Most stories and legends about caribou told of their benevolence. Charlie Peter Charlie, an elder of Old Crow, told me a story about a child in a hunting camp who was chronically sick to his stomach. While camp members were out hunting caribou, the child was left back at camp. As he was sitting on a rock watching for the people to return, a small caribou calf came up to him and licked his stomach. When the people returned a short time later, he was healed of his sickness and was healthy from then on.

An Inuit myth tells of a boy who was adopted by a great hunter, who taught

THROUGH RITUALS

AND TABOOS,

HUNTERS SHOWED

THE ANIMAL THAT

THEY HELD NO

MALICE TOWARDS

IT BUT SIMPLY

NEEDED TO EAT.

WHENEVER PEOPLE

SEE A WHITE CARIBOU

NOW THEY ARE CARE-

FUL NOT TO HARM IT,

BECAUSE IT MIGHT

HAVE THE SOUL OF A

YOUNG WOMAN.

him how to be a skillful hunter. One fall day, the boy was learning how to kill a caribou by hiding under a caribou skin with a knife around his waist. When he got close to the caribou, it spoke to him. He wondered if he were going mad. But the caribou told him, "Those of us who are to be leaders in the future have the gift to occasionally be able to lift the face mask of our people and speak on behalf of our people." He told the boy to put the skin on right and he would show him what to do. In this way, the boy became a caribou and lived with the caribou all winter, learning how to paw through the snow and what kind of food to eat. When they were migrating in the spring, he was shot in the neck with an arrow by another great hunter from another tribe. He crawled out of his caribou skin and was surprised to find his knife still tied around his waist. He joined that tribe and later became a great hunter and leader.

While performing an aerial photo census of the George River herd, I happened to photograph a pure white albino caribou. Later, when I showed the picture to John Mameamskum, a Cree of the Naskapi Band, near Schefferville, Quebec, he became excited and said that white caribou were highly revered, though he didn't explain why. I later read an Inuit myth that may shed some light on this mystery. The story tells of a young couple that had recently been married. One day, when the husband and his brothers were out hunting and the wife was in the igloo, a witch transformed her into a white caribou. She became scared and ran off with the caribou. When her husband returned and found her missing, he was very sad. His grandmother, who was a shaman, told him what had happened and gave him a sealskin bag. She told him to open the bag if he saw a white caribou and he would get his wife back. He travelled far and wide and finally found a herd of caribou that included a white caribou. He opened the bag, and a white weasel ran out and jumped on the caribou, knocking it down. The young wife got up from where the white caribou had fallen and came to her glad husband. Whenever people see a

FACING PAGE

Whereas white reindeer like this one are quite common, albino caribou occur very rarely. P.O. ERIKSSON/ NATUREPHOTOGRAPHERS IN SWEDEN

white caribou now they are careful not to harm it, because it might have the soul of a young woman.

In the summer, when caribou are gathered into just a few large aggregations, most of the summer range is completely empty. In the 1970s, when radio collars were not yet reliable enough to use over such huge areas, biologists had to find these large groups by using tracking skills and luck, just as hunters did, except that the biologists had planes to help. People in planes can scan the huge and virtually empty summer range for fresh trails much faster than the hunters ever could, but the herds still often evaded the biologists. When the hunters did find the herds in their summer groups, there was a flood of caribou rushing over the ground.

I often wondered how the indigenous people could find such groups. This story, told by Pierre Judas of Snare Lake with a bit of humour, describes their frustration and the methods they used. One time when people could not find any caribou and were very hungry, they often saw a raven flying overhead and wondered why he looked so strong if there were no caribou around. The raven was not telling of any caribou, but the people did not trust him. They decided to use their medicine to track the raven. One shaman used his medicine to discover that the raven was hiding all the caribou. Another transformed himself into a fox to follow the raven and found the raven's tent full of live caribou. The raven had a fire by the door, and when the fox went inside his tail caught on fire. In the confusion that followed, the caribou stampeded out of the shelter, trampling the raven to death and leaving nothing but feathers scattered on the ground. The raven was special to the people, so they used their medicine to bring him back to life again. They scolded the raven and told him he must share the caribou with everyone. Hunters now never wear fox fur when they are hunting caribou because they believe that as a result of this experience caribou still run from the fox.

Two mature males and a young male are properly dressed for the formal dance of the mating season.
MICHAEL S. QUINTON

The Inuit believed they had two souls. One soul was visible and physical and animated the person. This soul was not reincarnated but went off to the happy place in the sky when the person died. The other soul, the name soul, was free-floating and was like a guardian angel. It was invisible and private and would be reincarnated into any newborn child with the same name. It could be shared if the older person was still alive when a newborn was named. Animal souls were also free-floating and would re-associate with another animal for the hunter to hunt again only if he observed the correct rituals and taboos. If he didn't show such respect, the animal soul would not associate with another animal for him to hunt.

The Inuit used the trick of acting

in a strange manner, such as

writhing and flopping around

on the ground, to

evoke the curiosity

of the caribou and

cause them to come

closer, within the

range of the bows

and arrows.

RESPECTFUL USE

Caribou were normally abundant and satisfied basic needs such as food, shelter and clothing for people of the North. Parts of their bodies could also be made into many other supplies, such as needles and bags (for carrying food, water and tools), as well as weapons.

Before they had guns, northern cultures employed many ingenious methods to catch and kill caribou. The Inuit used the trick of acting in a strange manner, such as writhing and flopping around on the ground, to evoke the curiosity of the caribou and cause them to come closer, within the range of the bows and arrows. Such weapons were fashioned from caribou antler, muskox horn, flint and sinew, a string or thread spun from the tendons on the backs of mammals. The Inuit also used lines of *inukshuit*, the plural of *inukshuk*, which were rocks stacked on top of each other to look like people; the word *inukshuk* means "peoplelike."

These figures were built in lines, usually along ridges near routes that the caribou used, where they approached rivers, lakes or other favoured hunting sites. Used in conjunction with women and children who hazed the caribou along, these *inukshuit* increased the effectiveness of the real hazers, since the caribou responded to the images as well as to the women and children. In this way, the caribou were moved towards the hunters hiding behind blinds or waiting in kayaks at water crossings to spear the caribou while they were swimming.

These figures were often very realistic, even though they were made with just a few stones. Once when I was near our camp along a lakeshore, where I thought there was nobody near me, I was suddenly aware of someone very close. I turned and saw an Inuk sitting near the shore. Just as quickly I realized that it was a lone *inukshuk*, probably intended as a navigational aid during blizzards and whiteouts.

The Dene and Cree used snares of babiche, which was made from caribou skins with the hair removed. The skin was cut into narrow rawhide thongs, and several of these were twisted together to make a rope. The Dene and Cree also used bows, arrows and spears made of wood, sinew, flint and bone. These were fashioned, and used, with great skill. The snares were tied to trees and placed along paths in order to catch the caribou, usually by the antlers. They were also used in conjunction with fences leading to enclosures made of trees and shrubs tied together and fixed with roots. These enclosures were placed either on sloped land or on the ice on rivers and lakes and were designed to trap migrating caribou inside, using wing fences and a gate that was an obvious opening to the caribou as they entered but became invisible when they attempted to leave. Snares were placed along the inside walls of the enclosure. Because the enclosures were long and narrow, caribou that weren't snared could be speared or shot with arrows from outside the enclosure.

Some of these methods may seem cruel to modern sensibilities; we expect

An Inuit ivory carving of unknown date of a caribou bull. GLENBOW COLLECTION, CALGARY, ALBERTA, CANADA (IMAGE NO. CN: R2466-2)

ETHNOLOGISTS

ESTIMATE THAT IT

TOOK A MINIMUM

OF TWENTY CARIBOU

TO SUPPLY ONE

PERSON'S NEEDS

FOR FOOD AND

SUPPLIES FOR A

YEAR.

animals to die quickly as a result of modern technology, such as rifles and stun guns in slaughterhouses. But Native people did not have these methods, and they needed to eat. They had only the materials at hand and their own ingenuity to secure the nourishment required for their survival in this demanding land, where farming is impossible and only a few wild plants produce edible leaves, roots or fruits.

These Sámi bridal boots are made of caribou skin with the hair left on, wool and cotton. GLENBOW COLLECTION, CALGARY, ALBERTA, CANADA (IMAGE NO. CN: AB1099 A–B)

FACING PAGE

A Cree hunting coat decorated to please the caribou, thus increasing the hunter's chance of success. CANADIAN MUSEUM OF CIVILIZATION (IMAGE NO. S77-1856)

The people also used the caribou to make weapons, drums, thongs, containers, tents, sleeping bags and clothing, including moccasins. Ethnologists estimate that it took a minimum of twenty caribou to supply one person's needs for food and supplies for a year.

Since sealskin is waterproof and tough and caribou skin is warm, the Inuit preferred seal hide for the soles of their mukluks but often used caribou skin for the tops and liners. For winter clothing they used two layers of caribou clothing, with the hair left on. For the people in the far North who live and work in the open during the day and sleep in unheated tents at night, no modern textiles are warmer than caribou clothing. Caribou skin is superb for providing warm, soft sleeping mats and as a floor covering in a tent or igloo.

The Inuit included caribou in their varied art forms, from carvings to silk-screen prints to appliquéd wall hangings or banners. They also made carvings from caribou antlers. The antlers and bones and thongs were used in some of the games they played to avoid becoming depressed or out of shape during the long winters.

CARIBOU HAVE BEEN

AN IMPORTANT MAIN-

STAY OF NORTHERN

COMMUNITIES AND

WILL CONTINUE TO

BE SO.

The Montagnais and Naskapi of Quebec used the caribou skin in a similar way. The women also made hunting coats with the hair turned in and the hide facing outward, painted in elaborate designs. The designs were composed of different combinations of a fixed set of motifs and were extremely time-consuming to make. These coats provided the required magical or spiritual qualities to ensure a successful hunt for the wearer, usually the husband. The basic motifs came in the dreams of the hunter, who described them to his wife. He depended on her skill to paint the designs and spin the magic that would please the caribou so that they would come out of their Caribou Mountain House and generously give themselves to the hunter. Two coats had to be made each year, one for summer and one for winter. After a year the magic left the coat, and so a new one had to be crafted. The discarded coats could be traded to foreign travellers, adding to the wealth of both buyers and sellers. Fortunately, some of these magnificent coats, made to please the caribou, are preserved in museums.

Caribou have been an important mainstay of northern communities throughout the world for thousands of years and will continue to be so. They have gone through cycles of higher and lower numbers and will continue to go through these cycles. But if the habitat is not compromised by industry, if hunting is done with respect and if wolves are valued as partners in good management, caribou will be around for more years than can be counted.

PAGES 104–105

A summer snowstorm has caught these caribou in their light coats, but they are still comfortable. S. J. KRASEMANN/PETER ARNOLD, INC.

FACING PAGE

Part of the Porcupine caribou herd travels over the Arctic tundra. TONY DAWSON/WORDS & PICTURES

PAGES 108–109

Three migrating caribou females swim an Arctic river in an Alaskan sunset. TOM WALKER

NOTES

PART 1

pp. 1–2, 16.   E. C. Pielou, *After the Ice Age: The Return of Life to Glaciated North America* (Chicago: University of Chicago Press, 1991), 139.

pp. 2–3.   J. L. Davis, "Status of Rangifer in USA," in *Proceedings of 2nd International Reindeer/Caribou Symposium, Roros, Norway, 1979*, ed. E. Reiners, E. Gaare and S. Skjenneberg (Trondheim, Norway: Direktoratet for vilt og ferskvannsfisk, 1980), 793–97.

pp. 2–3.   George W. Calef, "Status of Rangifer in Canada," in *Proceedings of 2nd International Reindeer/Caribou Symposium, Roros, Norway, 1979*, ed. E. Reiners, E. Gaare and S. Skjenneberg (Trondheim, Norway: Direktoratet for vilt og ferskvannsfisk, 1980), 754–59.

pp. 2–3.   Don Russell (Canadian Wildlife Service, Whitehorse, Yukon), personal communications with the author about the most recent estimate of the size of the Porcupine herd, 1997.

pp. 2–3.   Mika Sutherland (Department of Renewable Resources, Northwest Territories), personal communications with the author about the most recent estimates of the four herds in the Northwest Territories (numbers 3, 4, 5 and 6 on the map), 1997.

pp. 2–3.   Serge Couturier (northern caribou biologist, Ministère de l'Environnement et de la Faune, Québec), personal communications with the author about the Leaf River herd, 1995.

pp. 2–3.   S. Couturier, R. Courtois, H. Crepeau, L-P. Rivest and S. Luttich, "Calving Photo Census of the Rivière George Caribou Herd and Comparison with an Independent Census," in *Proceedings of the Sixth North American Caribou Workshop, Prince George, B.C., March 1994* (*Rangifer* Special Issue No. 9), ed. Dent Brown et al. (Tromso, Norway: Nordic Council for Reindeer Research, 1996), 283–96. *Rangifer* is a scientific journal that includes only material on the genus *Rangifer*; it is published by the Nordic Council for Reindeer Research.

pp. 2–3.   E. Reimers, L. Villmo, E. Garre, V. Holthe and T. Skogland, "Status of Rangifer in Norway Including Svalbard," in *Proceedings of 2nd International Reindeer/Caribou Symposium, Roros, Norway, 1979*, ed. E. Reiners, E. Gaare and S. Skjenneberg (Trondheim, Norway: Direktoratet for vilt og ferskvannsfisk, 1980), 774–85.

pp. 2–3, 11.   D. R. Seip and D. B. Cichowski, "Population Ecology of Caribou in British Columbia," in *Proceedings of the Sixth North American Caribou Workshop, Prince George, B.C., March 1994* (*Rangifer* Special Issue No. 9), ed. Dent Brown et al. (Tromso, Norway: Nordic Council for Reindeer Research, 1996), 73–80. This article includes information about the diet of woodland caribou.

pp. 2–3, 22.   B. M. Pavlov, L. A. Kolpashchikov and V. A. Zyryanov, "Population Dynamics of the Taimyr Reindeer Population," in *Proceedings of the Sixth North American Caribou Workshop, Prince George, B.C., March 1994* (*Rangifer* Special Issue No. 9), ed. Dent Brown et al. (Tromso, Norway: Nordic Council for Reindeer Research, 1996), 381–84.

pp. 2–3, 22.   V. M. Safronov, "Wild Reindeer of Yakutia," in *Proceedings of the Sixth North American Caribou Workshop, Prince George, B.C., March 1994* (*Rangifer* Special Issue No. 9), ed. Dent Brown et al. (Tromso, Norway: Nordic Council for Reindeer Research, 1996), 387–89.

pp. 2–3, 22.   Vladimir Mosolov, "Wild Reindeer of the Kamchatka Peninsula," in *Proceedings of the Sixth North American Caribou Workshop, Prince George, B.C., March 1994* (*Rangifer* Special Issue No. 9), ed. Dent Brown et al. (Tromso, Norway: Nordic Council for Reindeer Research, 1996), 385–86.

pp. 5–8.   Frank L. Miller, *Peary Caribou Status Report* (Edmonton: Environment Canada, Canadian Wildlife Service, Western and Northern Region, 1990). This 64-page report was prepared for the Committee on the Status of Endangered Wildlife in Canada.

p. 12.   Gerald D. Racey and Edward R. Armstrong, "Towards a Caribou Habitat Management Strategy for Northwestern Ontario: Running the Gauntlet," in *Proceedings of the Sixth North American Caribou Workshop, Prince George, B.C., March 1994* (*Rangifer* Special Issue No. 9), ed. Dent Brown et al. (Tromso, Norway: Nordic Council for Reindeer Research, 1996), 159–69.

p. 12.   Mary MacNutt, "Saving the Woodland Caribou," *Globe and Mail*, 31 January 1995.

pp. 13–15.   E. Janet Edmunds and Kirby G. Smith, *Mountain Caribou Calf Production and Survival, and Calving and Summer Habitat Use in West-Central Alberta* (Wildlife Research Series No. 4) (Edmonton: Alberta Forestry, Lands and Wildlife, Fish and Wildlife, 1991).

p. 15.   E. Terry, B. McLellan, G. Watts and J. Flaa, "Early Winter Habitat Use by Mountain Caribou in the North Caribou and Columbia Mountains, British Columbia," in *Proceedings of the Sixth North American Caribou Workshop, Prince George, B.C., March 1994* (*Rangifer* Special Issue No. 9), ed. Dent Brown et al. (Tromso, Norway: Nordic Council for Reindeer Research, 1996), 133–40.

p. 16.   Mark O'Donoghue (wildlife biologist, Wildlife Division of the Government of Newfoundland and Labrador), personal communications with the author, 1997.

pp. 24–25.   Hans Staaland (Department of Biology and Nature Conservation, Agricultural University of Norway), personal communications with the author, 1997.

p. 32.   T. Ringberg, K. Nilssen and E. Strom, "Do Svalbard Reindeer Use Subcutaneous Fat as Insulation?" in *Proceedings of 2nd International Reindeer/Caribou Symposium, Roros, Norway, 1979*, ed. E. Reiners, E. Gaare and S. Skjenneberg (Trondheim, Norway: Direktoratet for vilt og ferskvannsfisk, 1980), 392–95. This study concluded that Svalbard reindeer do not use subcutaneous fat as insulation, depending on their hair alone.

PART 2

p. 34.   V. A. Langman and C. R. Taylor, "Nasal Heat Exchange in a Northern Ungulate, the Reindeer (*Rangifer tarandus*)," in *Proceedings of 2nd International Reindeer/Caribou Symposium, Roros, Norway, 1979,* ed. E. Reiners, E. Gaare and S. Skjenneberg (Trondheim, Norway: Direktoratet for vilt og ferskvannsfisk, 1980), 377.

p. 85.   R. A. Wales, L. R. Miligan and I. McEvean, "Urea Recycling in Caribou, Cattle and Sheep," in *1st Proceedings of International Caribou-Reindeer Symposium* (University of Alaska Special Report No. 1) (Fairbanks: University of Alaska, 1975), 297–307.

PART 3

p. 93.   F. Mowat, *Never Cry Wolf* (Boston: Little, Brown, 1963). Mowat's friend Ootek is the source of this creation myth.

p. 96.   The only source I found for the white caribou was at the following website: www.bcommox.net/~mbuchanan/realm/inuit

pp. 98, 101.   E. Hall, ed., *People and Caribou, in the Northwest Territories* (Yellowknife, N.W.T.: Department of Renewable Resources, Northwest Territories, 1989) describes caribou snares and fences, and the uses Inuit and Dene people made of caribou carcasses (pp. 11–41). Donald Kaglik's story of the boy who became a caribou is on pp. 55–57; Pierre Judas's story "The Raven and the Caribou" is on pp. 59–60.

p. 99.   In *Issumatug: Learning from the Traditional Helping Wisdom of the Canadian Inuit* (Halifax: Fernwood Publishers, 1992), Kit Minor describes the two souls of Inuit and the one of animals.

p. 106.   Dorothy K. Burnham, *To Please the Caribou: Painted Caribou-Skin Coats Worn by the Naskapi, Montagnais, and Cree Hunters of the Quebec-Labrador Peninsula* (Toronto: Royal Ontario Museum, 1992).

FOR FURTHER READING

Calef, George W. *Caribou and the Barren Lands.* Ottawa: Canadian Arctic Resources Committee/Toronto: Foxfire Books, 1981. This popular book is as current as when it was published.

Hall, E., ed. *People and Caribou, in the Northwest Territories.* Yellowknife, N.W.T.: Department of Renewable Resources, Northwest Territories, 1989.

Miller, D. S., and J. Van Zyle. *A Caribou Journey.* Boston: Little, Brown, 1994. For younger readers.

INDEX